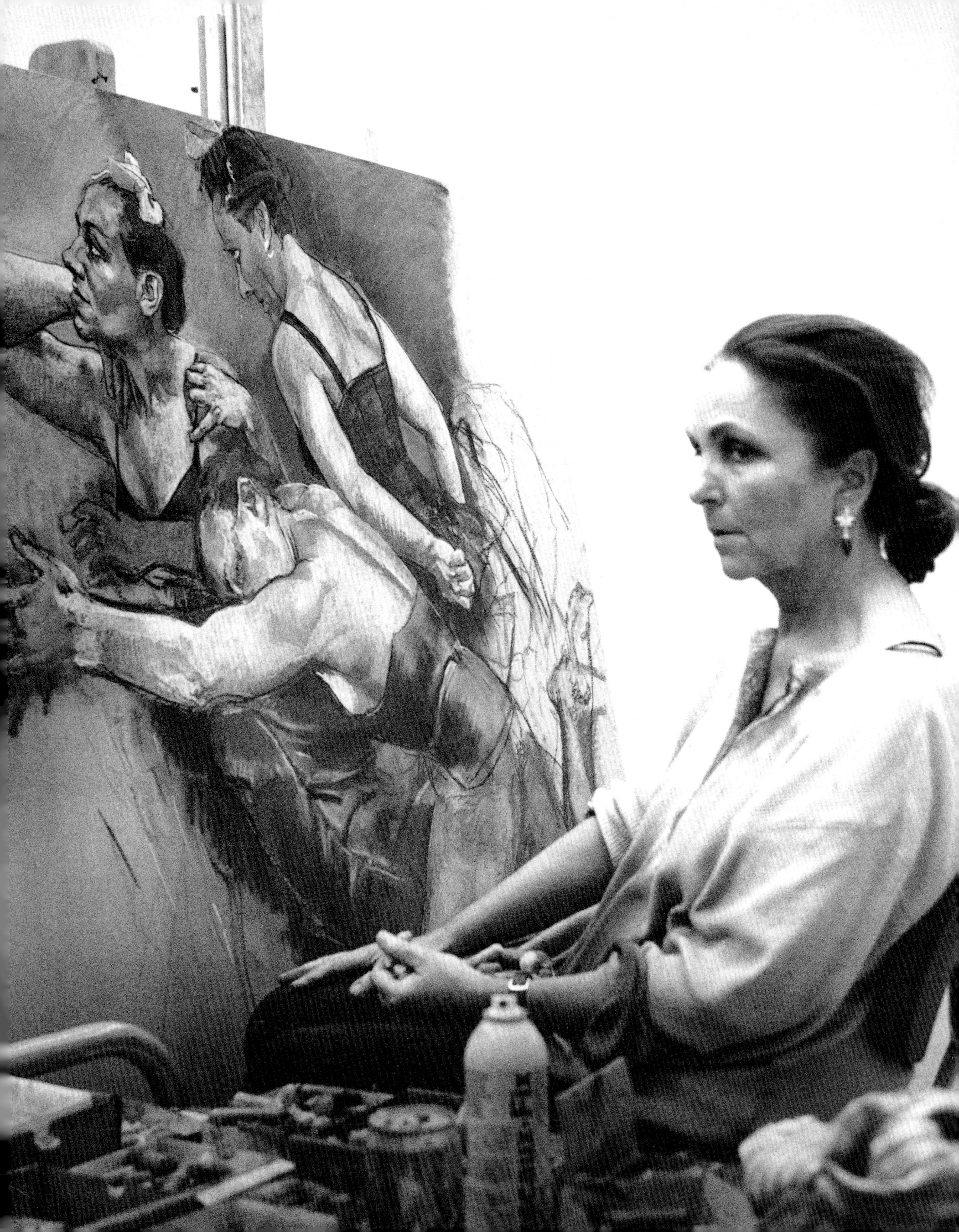

PAULA REGO

THE DANCING OSTRICHES FROM DISNEY'S 'FANTASIA'

INTRODUCTION
Sarah Kent

ESSAY
John McEwen

SAATCHI COLLECTION

INTRODUCTION

'MUTTON DRESSED AS LAMB: PAULA REGO'S OSTRICH WOMEN'

Sarah Kent

'Mutton dressed as lamb' is a cruel saying, a double put-down. It confirms the status of women as meat, while ridiculing older specimens for trying to retain their place in the meat market – for resisting consignment to the knacker's yard, and appealing for love and affection.

Crammed into skimpy black tutus and pink ballet pumps, Paula Rego's Ostrich women are the embodiment of the phrase. Neither satin bodices nor frothy tulle skirts can make their lumpen bodies seem girlish, slim or graceful. The skimpy costumes cannot conceal the beefy thighs, strong backs, thick necks and muscular arms of people used to the tough work of cooking, cleaning and carrying. These are nature women – mothers and grandmothers for whom romance is mainly a memory, or a sensation of longing. Their resigned expressions suggest that they no longer expect much fun from life.

Two groups are clustered as though waiting in the wings to go on stage. One group faces left the other right, as though confronting one another. The matrons on the right seem somewhat wary and defensive, those on the left are hitching up their skirts as though spoiling for a fight. The figures stand on a white ground, but are ranged above one another like angels banked up on the clouds of a Tintoretto melodrama. If they were not all dressed in black, one might imagine them to be the forces of good and evil, eyeing one another across the heavens of some turbulent Last Judgement.

The other six pastels in the series show individuals resting or limbering up in preparation for their cue. Whether slumped on the floor or propped up with cushions, their heavy bodies and ungainly movements are a gruesome travesty of the lightness and elegance of ballerinas.

If Rego's dancers are merely piteous, we could jeer at them with smug self-satisfaction and retain our prejudices intact. But her gallumphing heroines are not simply a laughing-stock; there is too much empathy and pathos in their characterisation. These overblown performers arouse as much sympathy as ridicule, and ambush the assumptions that prop up our prejudices.

The pastels are based on Rego's recollections of the ostriches who cavort to classical music in Walt Disney's film *Fantasia*. The cartoon made me uncomfortable, even as a child. I had the uneasy feeling that it demeaned the birds and animals portrayed, the dancers they mimicked and the music that accompanied their girations. I find ballerinas problematic anyway; they embody such a wealth of contradictions. Young women undergo strenuous training, while starving themselves in order to retain the pre-pubescent bodies necessary to wear garments more appropriate for fairies than real females. On stage, difficult movements are made to seem effortless by performers who, in assuming the roles of wilting heroines, belie their own skills and status.

The image that, for me, embodies these discrepancies is a bruised and bleeding foot clad in a white satin pump – almost as fetishistic in its masking of reality as a bound foot housed in a dainty slipper.

If Rego's full-bodies women look foolish in their tutus, this says as much about the dresses they are crammed into as their desire to be slim and nubile. I am amazed at our willingness to conform to dress codes, no matter how inappropriate. A few years ago every function was attended by middle-aged women wearing puff-ball party dresses more suited to young schoolgirls. So as not to look ridiculous in their little, thigh-length frocks, the wearers starved themselves to a scrawny approximation of adolescence. Rego's ostriches exemplify the longing to be young and desirable that drives mature women to absurd extremes.

Degas is an obvious point of reference for Rego's dancers. He was accused of mysogeny because he portrayed ballerinas as hard-working women, rather than beautiful phantoms, and went behind the scenes to show them exercising at the bar, rehearsing, dressing, waiting in the wings or slumped in exhaustion after the show. By depicting them in odd or ungainly poses, he demystified the dancers not, I think, to belittle them (as many have claimed), but to release them from the bondage of collective fantasy so that they could reclaim reality.

Whereas Degas' drawings are mainly documentary, Rego's pastels are emblematic. A solitary dancer, perched on crumpled cushions as though posing for a photo-call, seems unaware of the discrepancy between her stocky build and the slender proportions expected of a dancer. Another stretches her arms forward in a gesture more akin to a plea for affection than a balletic pose. Both are unlikely to awaken the desired response, and therein lies the comedy and the tragedy of these muscular maidens.

Why ostriches? Women are often nicknamed after birds – hen, duck or chick if they are young and amenable; goose, harpy or albatross if old or demanding. Rego's women embody the absurdity of all such associations. The issue is one of dignity. Implicit in these icons of unseemly striving is a plea to be valued for what you are, and not be made to jump through hoops or don ludicrous guises in order to gain attention.

"The time of day in that place, of that climate, has the presence of an animal. A heavy, uneasy, sun-baked thing which twitters and whines in one's ear. One must tease it, humiliate it, gouge it, pity it. The picture becomes its face. If it can be described it can be forgiven for being what is is and made loveable even. Such creatures (fawning, lethargic, elusive) rush about or wander, lost, singly and even in packs. For Paula, painting is trapping them, breaking them, putting on brands and hanging them, groomed and pampered, on the wall."

Victor Willing

Published anonymously in the catalogue to the exhibition 'Six Painters' at the Institute of Contemporary Arts, London, 1966.

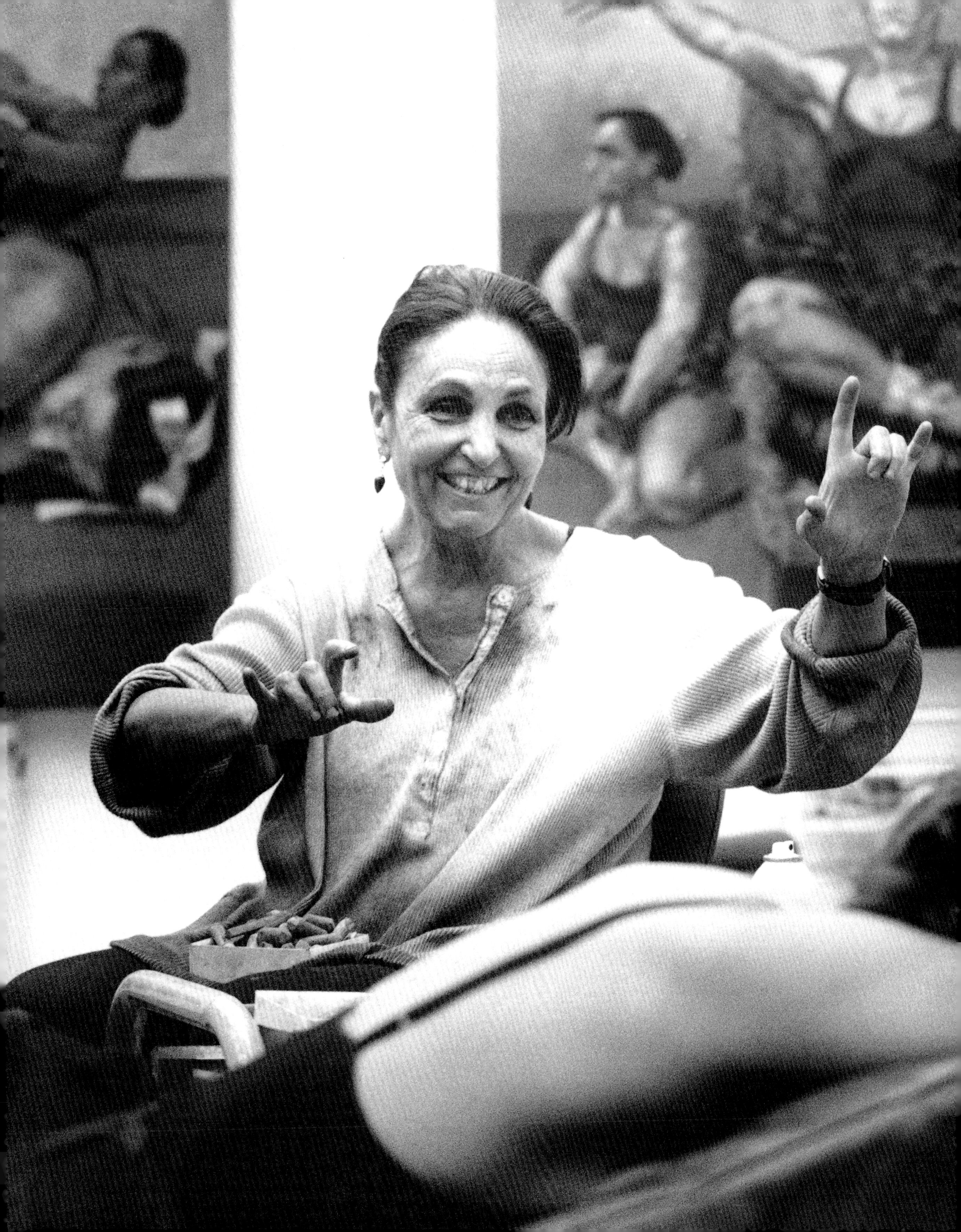

THE OSTRICHES: A TRIBE OF BIRD WOMEN ON THE EDGE OF THE SEA

John McEwen

"It's all there! It's all in that piece Vic wrote and I never realized it till I read it again just now!" Paula Rego announced excitedly over the telephone, referring to the cycle of eight large pastels uniformly entitled *The Ostriches*. The artist Victor Willing, her husband, whose paintings are also in the Saatchi Collection, died in 1988.

It *is* all there. The sense of brooding heat, the sturdy Portuguese women (' fawning, lethargic, elusive') – because Rego is first and last a Portuguese artist – and yearning. "One thing's for sure," says Rego, "*The Ostriches* couldn't have been done if I hadn't been the age I am. A younger woman wouldn't know what it was like; longing for things that are not gone, because they're inside one, but that are inaccessible."

For Rego there is something 'very ancient' about the ostrich women: "Very ancient in the story-telling sense. Like the Greek tragedies, it happened many centuries ago and still goes on. As animals they've been born knowing what to do, but they also have an animal's innocence."

They are Harpies, Homer's personified storm winds who carry the unprepared into oblivion. In the dog women series, which preceded them, there was always a story, a male presence implied though never seen. But with *The Ostriches* there is no story; no man (or child) is present or implied. The ostrich women may tempt or pursue men, but these are pictures of states of mind rather than narration; the most 'abstract', in the imaginative sense, of her career so far.

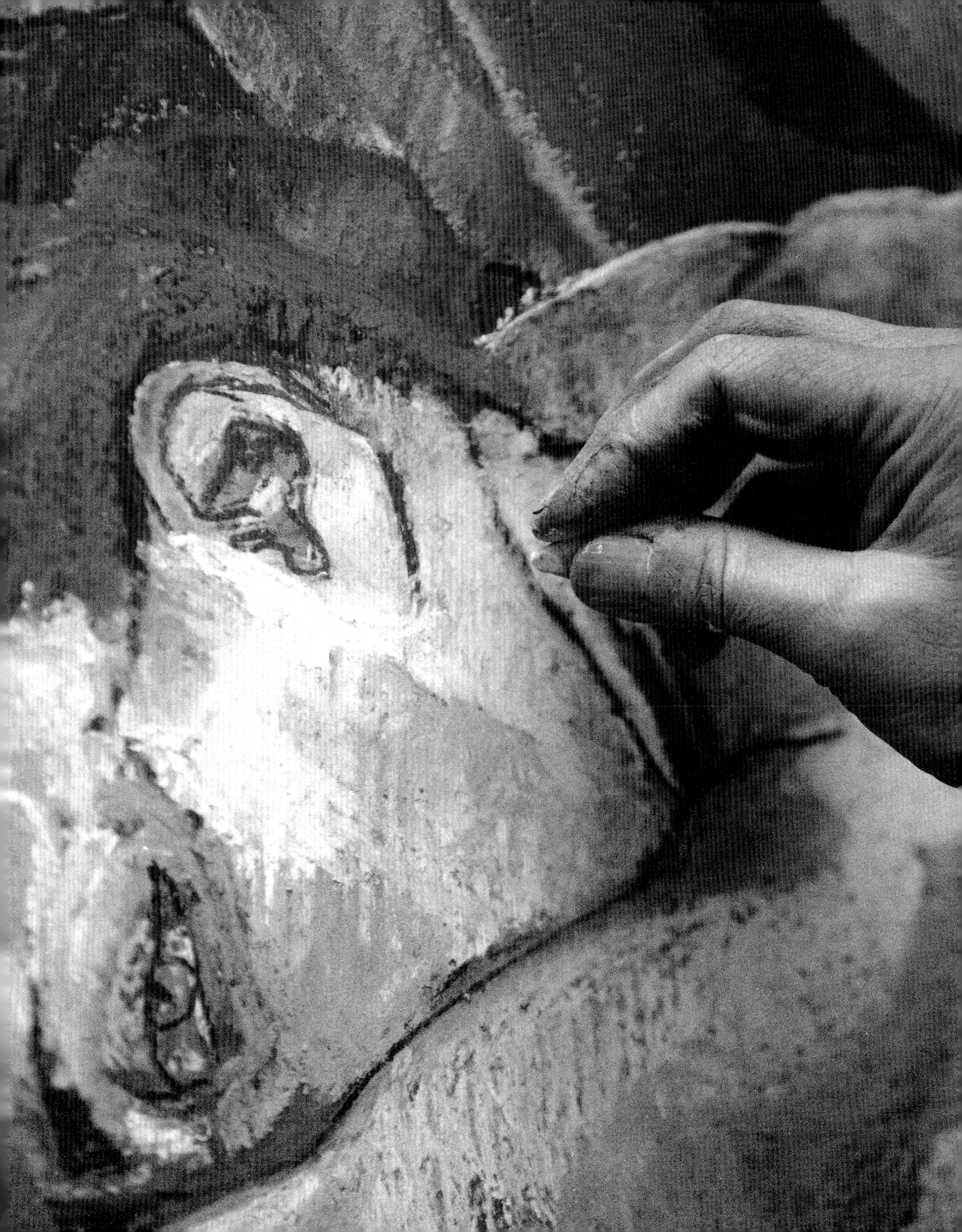

"I don't think there's much happiness in these pictures," says Lila Nunes, who being Portuguese nevertheless recognises their ferocity, "Some of them would eat you up. They even go out looking. The sleeping one is the safest." Her opinion of a recent article on *The Ostriches* is indicative: "Not bad, considering the writer wasn't Portuguese." Even the light in the pictures seems Portuguese, a storm light fit for Harpies, though they were drawn in Camden Town and done for 'Spellbound', an exhibition at the Hayward Gallery in spring 1996 to mark the centenary of British cinema.

The idea of contributing to the show immediately appealed to Rego, as Disney has been an artistic influence and inspiration ever since she first sat thrilled and terrified through *Snow White* as a child. For 'Spellbound' she contributed pictures inspired by three of her favourite Disney films – *Snow White, Pinocchio* and *Fantasia*. It was *Fantasia* she concentrated on, the most abstract of Disney's films, his interpretation of famous pieces of classical music through animation.

Rego purposely did not look at the film but relied on her memory and an occasional glance at John Cluhane's illustrated history of *Fantasia*. In the film the ostriches perform the waking or 'Morning' sequence from *Dance of the Hours*, a ballet in the opera *La Gioconda* (The Smiling One) by Amilcare Ponchielli, first performed in 1876. Cluhane writes that in the first stages the animators made sketches of ballet dancers who were brought to the studio to perform positions and movements, "the equivalent of a model's holding poses for an artist who draws still pictures." The models were turned into birds, sometimes quite literally. As those present recalled there was "a very tall, very ostrichlike girl, and she loved doing the burlesque of the ostrich for us... We put a few feathers on her costume where ostrich feathers should appear, and a bow on her head, and she performed the routine to perfection." Rego reverses this process, turning the birds back into people.

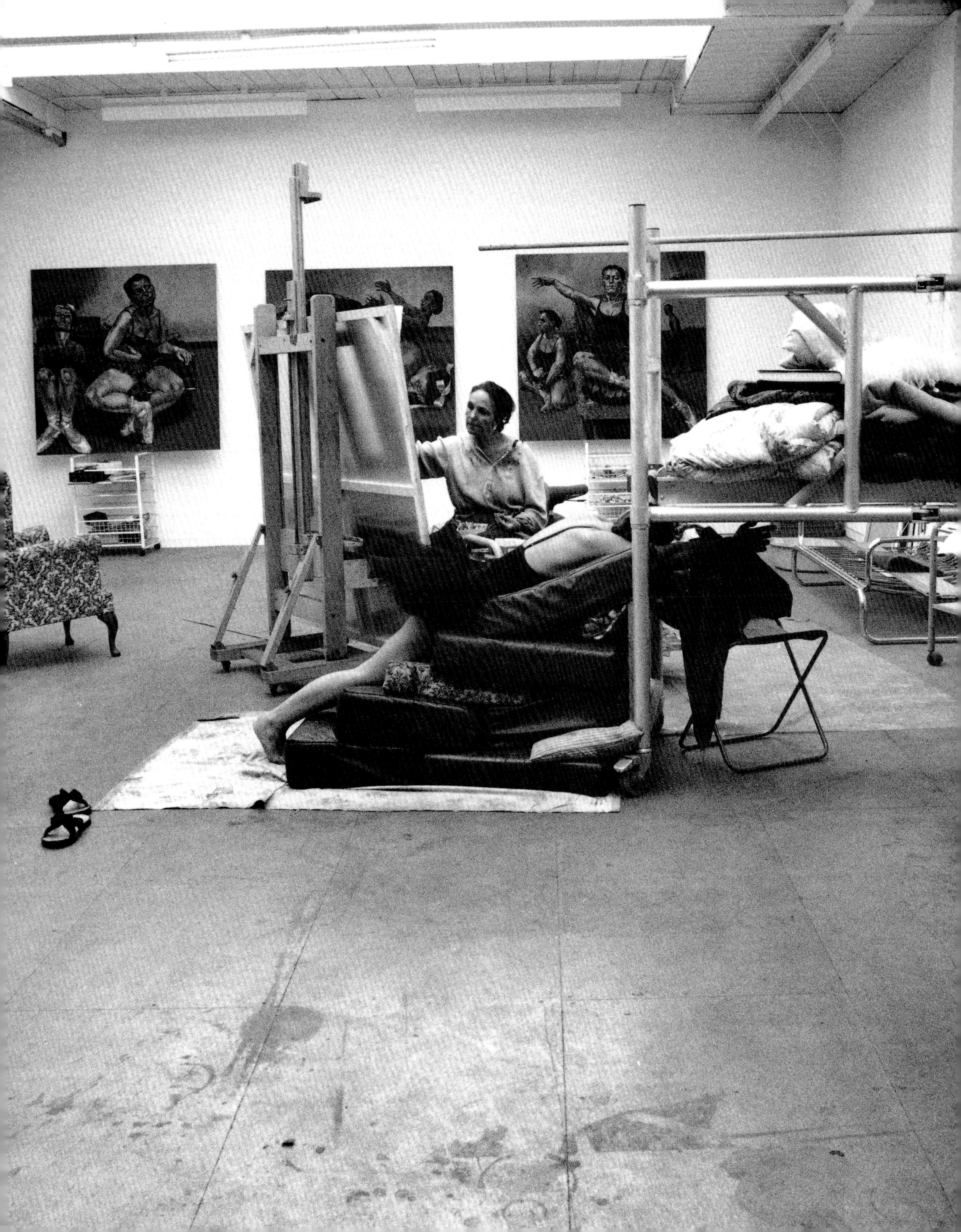

Lila Nunes, who has known the Willing family since she first came to nurse Victor Willing, has modelled for numerous Rego pictures. As she had done for the dog women, Rego drew the finished pictures for *The Ostriches* direct from Nunes' poses. This made the work especially collaborative, requiring improvisation on both sides.

"Lila has been living with my mother's fantasies for so many years that she can now add a little extra to them," says Nicholas Willing, Rego's son - himself an award-winning animator and film director. "Lila and she are very alike in their Portugueseness. It's a question of humour, a certain toughness and blunt lack of sentimentality." Using Nunes for all the ostrich women turns the eight pictures into eight frames of one figure. That is why the series only truly makes sense as one work, one woman displaying a range of emotions and positions but so changed in the drawing, only those who know Nunes well would recognise it. The sequential order tallies with the film, the ostriches waking up and proceeding to dance.

After a hilarious morning selecting clothes at a specialist shop for dancers, where the shopkeeper was puzzled by their total ignorance of dress and shoe sizes, Rego and Nunes returned to the studio. "This chair is always in the middle of the studio and I just sat on it and Paula asked me to put my arms up and she did a drawing," recalls Nunes. From there, in Rego's words, "the work took on a life of its own."

Drawing transports Rego back into a childlike frame of mind because, as an only child, it was her chief solace. With *The Ostriches* she became so engrossed she soon discarded preliminary studies to draw Nunes directly. Awkward positions of neck, arms or legs were supported by cushions, props sometimes included in the picture. Nunes is assimilated rather than portrayed. Sometimes her head is replaced by another; and one or two different characters creep in, particularly in the backgrounds. The ostrich women are made stockier, emphasising their ludicrous attempts to defy age and gravity, to 'fly'.

There is caustic, bucolic, peasant, even black humour in this; that fine line between comedy and tragedy. "Ballet, of course, is an abstraction in the way of movement, of story telling," Cluhane quotes T. Hee, director of the 'Hours' sequence. "Chaplin often said that he walked a tightrope with comedy on one side and tragedy on the other; if he tipped to one side, it would be tragedy; if he tipped to the other side, it would be comedy." Nicholas Willing's first reaction on seeing *The Ostriches* was to burst out laughing: "I thought they were the funniest things I'd ever seen. I laughed for a very long time and she laughed too – it was surprise and recognition all at once."

What he recognised was that world of make believe, so often inspired by films, of the film-fan wanting not just to act Snow White or James Bond, but to be them. The ostrich women are trying – repeatedly, exhaustingly – to be what they never can be. Even when they are together they act in isolation, doing their own thing. Some stalk in the distance, others flop or close their eyes and dream their dreams, waiting their turn.

For Rego the figures are grotesque, a word she is careful to distinguish from caricature. Caricature is mockery; grotesque, derived from grotto, describes the dark, secret, vulnerable side of human character. Like a middle-aged aerobics class the ostrich women strive heroically against increasing odds. 'They are old fighters', which is why one falls not like the dying swan in the ballet but the sculpture of the Gallic warrior in Rome: and why others form the heraldic prow of a ship, battling through the waves.

Part of their heroism, and of the force of the pictures, is the way they admit to feelings. "*The Ostriches* are founded in very deep feeling. They are the result of going through a lot of feelings and getting to the essence of them," says Nunes. "I have these feelings but I'm younger and they're mixed up. Paula concentrates many feelings. It's all very connected. Maybe most people don't acknowledge certain feelings, maybe that's why they can become more difficult as they get older.

Feelings almost too dark to speak of. I think women accept their feelings more than men. They're more open about them, they talk more about them with each other. A man will say: 'Everything's fine' when it isn't." This may explain why the adverse criticism of Rego's pictures has come exclusively from men.

Ideally the two drawings crowded with figures should be hung to make a doorway, a prelude to the rest. They can be interpreted equally as a chorus of ostrich women or one on her own displaying a range of postures and emotions. The left-side of the diptych describes spontaneous movement, with each figure using her dress as a prop, like actors improvising. One hides her head in shame, another holds her dress out like a net, several cradle the folds into bouquets or babies, perhaps even a dead baby in one guilty case. In the corner a vulgar duo do not seem to act at all. One leans on her thighs while to her rear the other rudely uses her dress as a handkerchief, to hold or blow her nose.

In the second drawing the mood is more subdued with even a hint of nemesis or death, the rustling flock becalmed in various attitudes of exhausted anticipation. Is our time up? Asks one, through the wistful inclination of her head. Of course it is! Says a prostrate form. The manly figure on the right stands defiantly, a toreador about to face the bull; in contrast to the gesticulating lady, determined to go down in style, or the figure closest to the light source waiting in the wings, shades of a Degas dancer.

There is a particular Iberian quality, *duende*, a combination of 'soul' and 'fatalism', which has no exact equivalent in English. To say a person has duende is the highest compliment. Can middle-aged women do ballet? Margot Fonteyn did. A person with duende can do anything at any age, so a lady with duende can dance anything at any time. I asked Rego if the ostrich women had duende. "They have," she said, grudgingly, "now and again." But *The Ostriches*, that is surely a masterpiece of duende.

THE DANCING OSTRICHES FROM DISNEY'S 'FANTASIA'

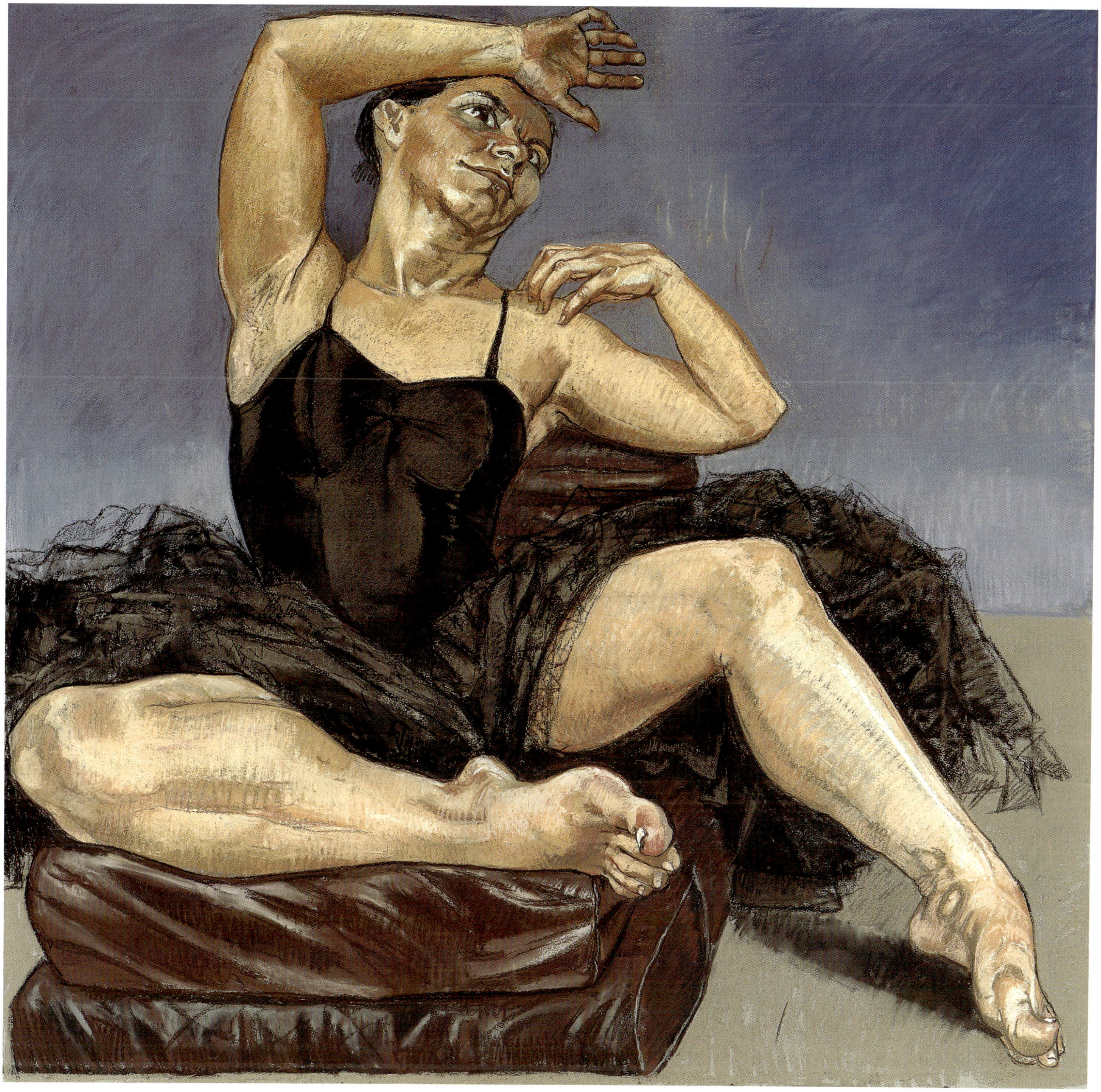

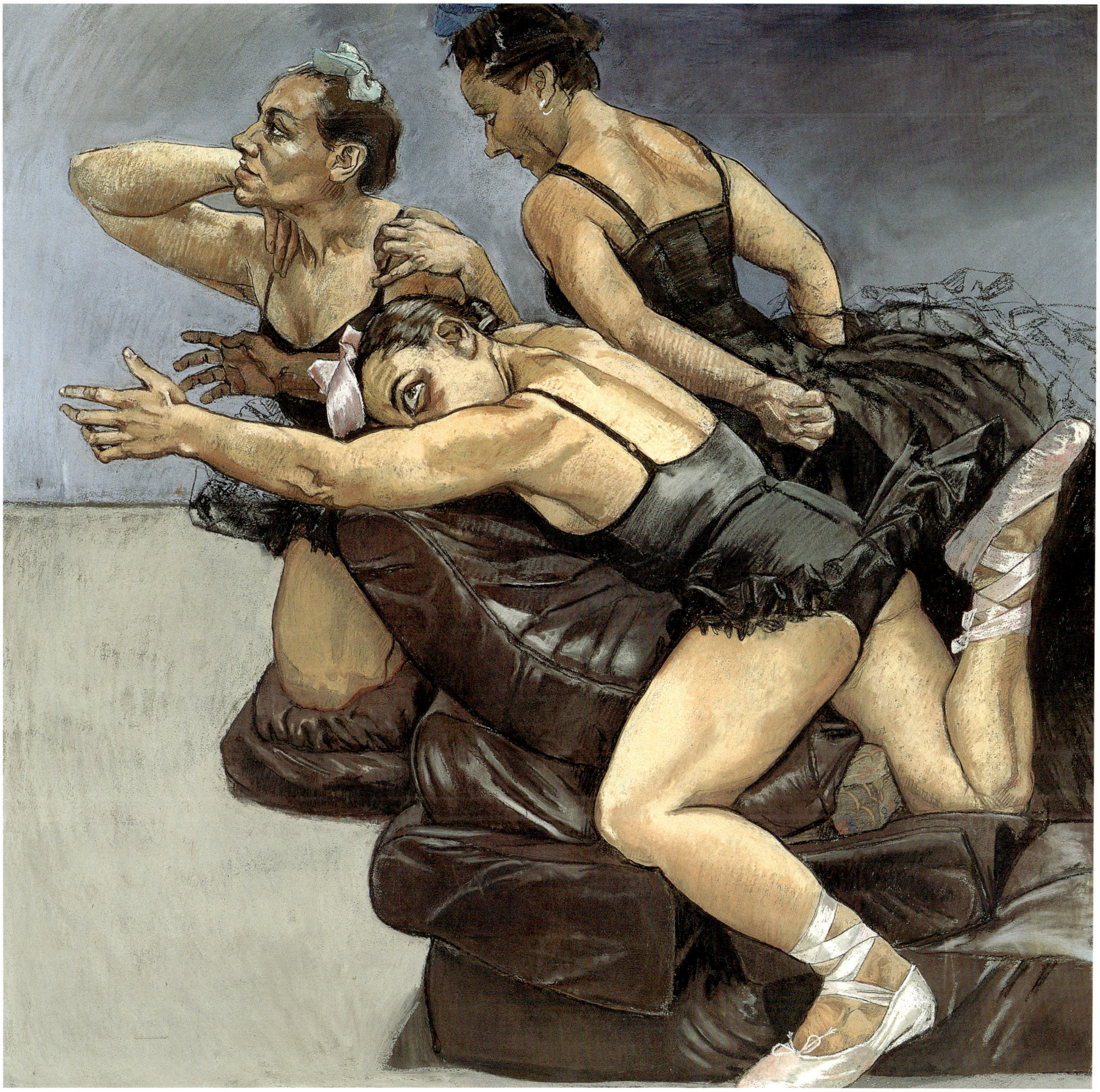

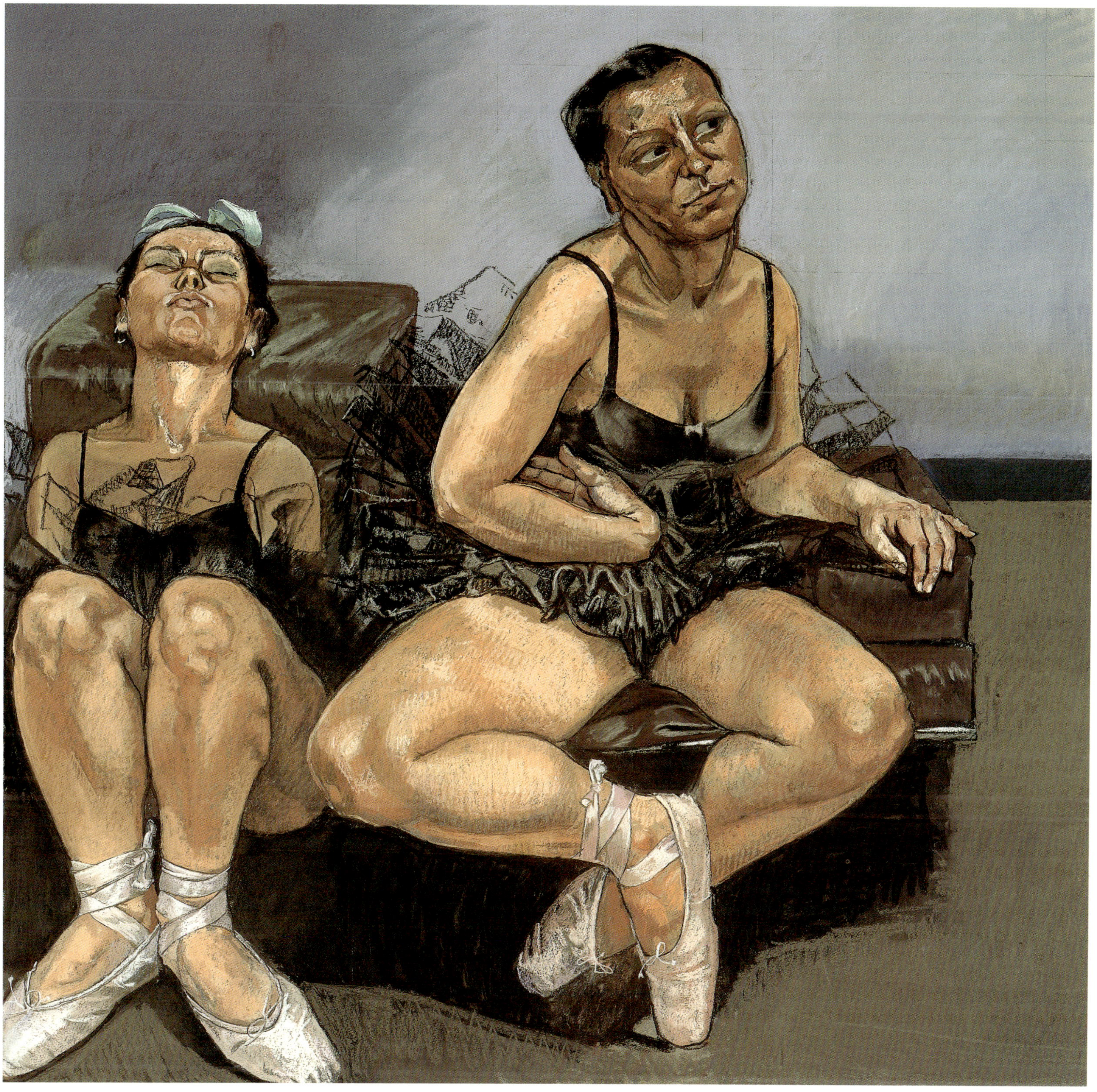

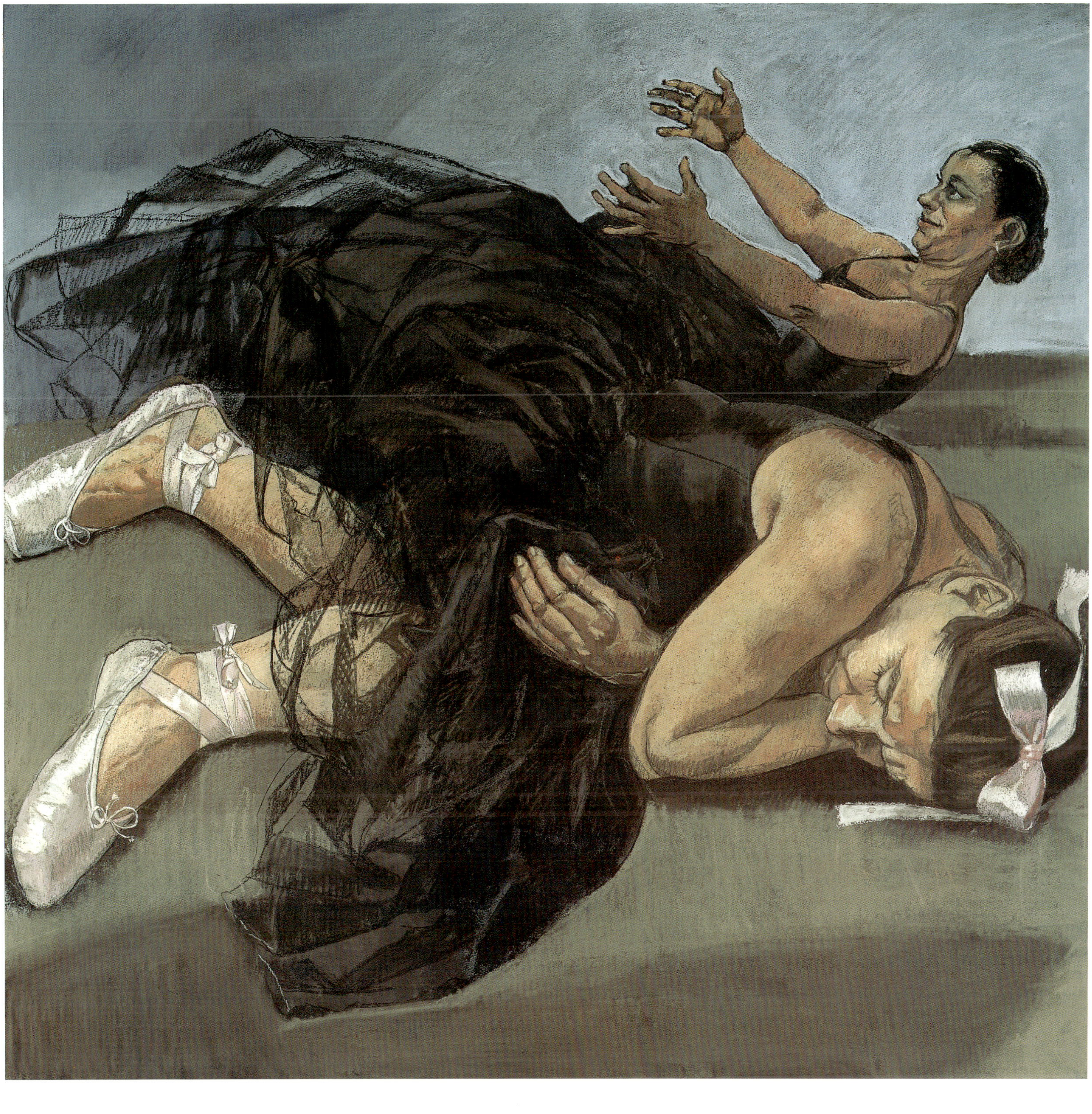

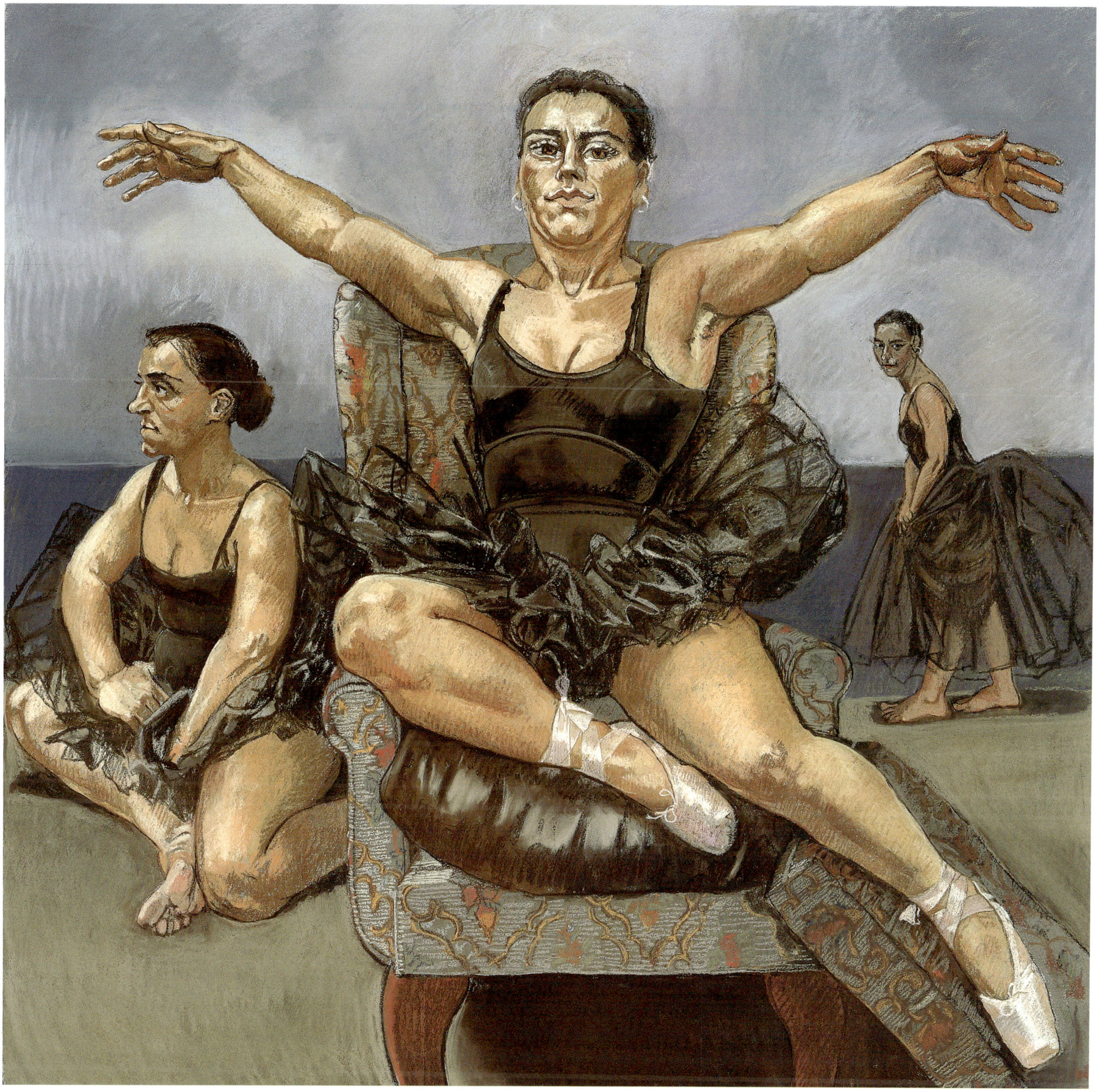

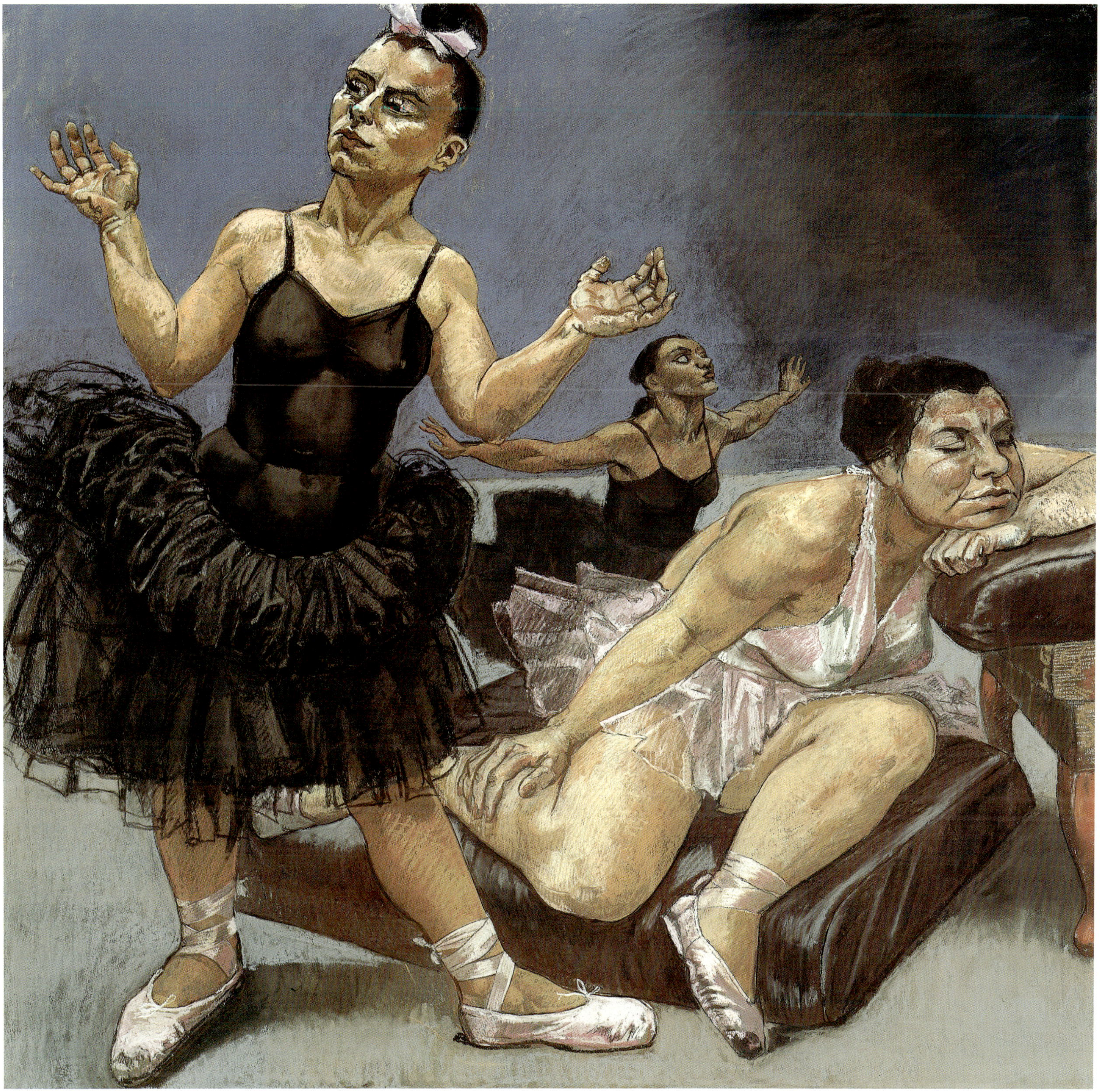

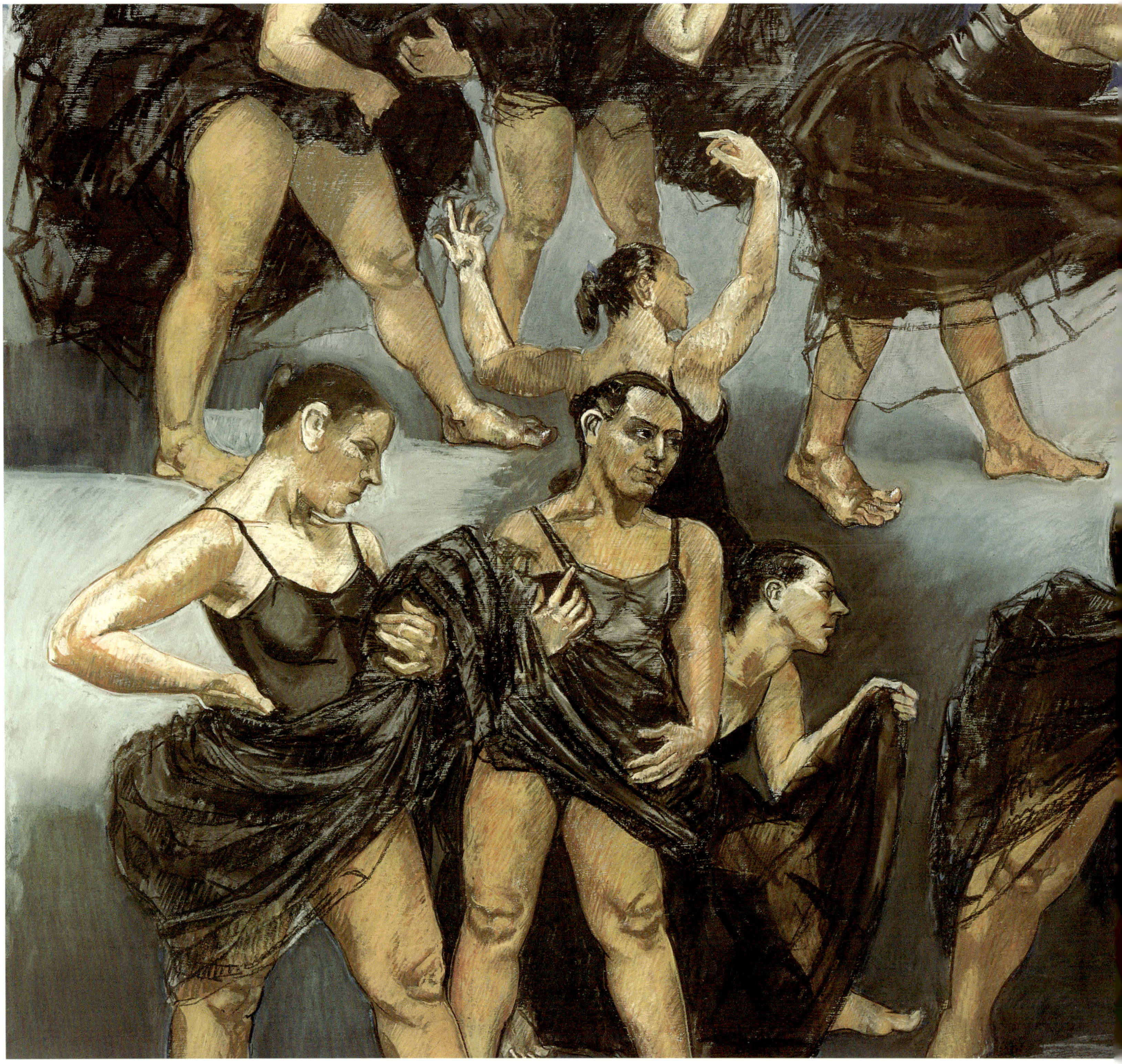

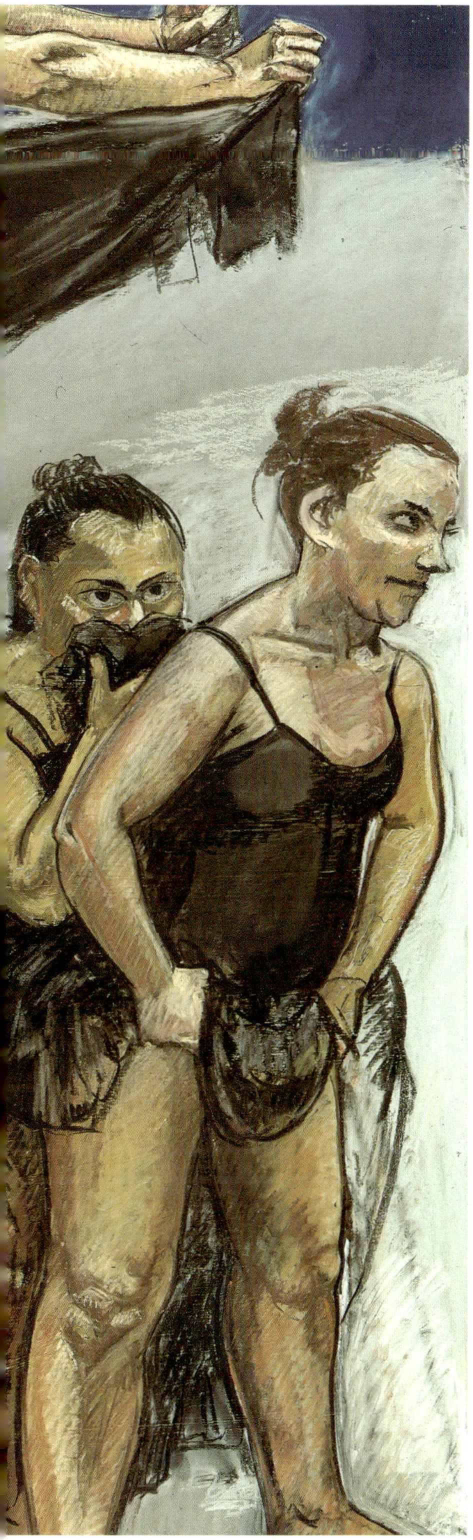
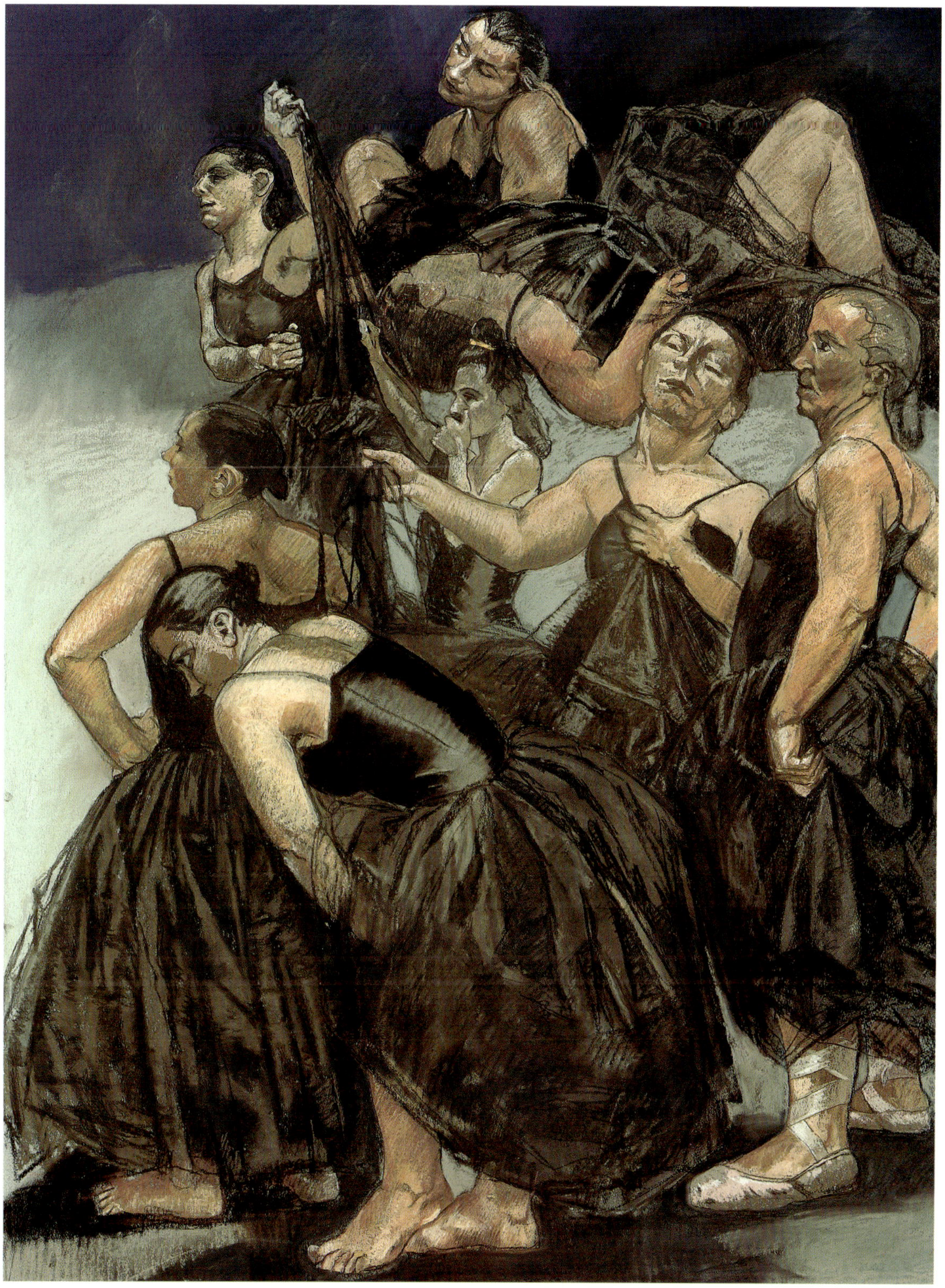

DANCING OSTRICHES FROM DISNEY'S 'FANTASIA'
1995

pastel on paper mounted on aluminium

(1 - 6) 59 x 59ins (150 x 150cm)

(7 - 8) Left: 63¾ x 61ins (162 x 155cm) Right: 63 x 47¼ins (160 x 120cm)

BIOGRAPHY

1935 — 26 January. Maria Paula Figueiroa Rego born in Lisbon, the first and only child of José Fernandes and Maria de S. José Avanti Quaresma Paiva Figueiroa Rego.

1937 — Her parents in England, where her father works in Chelmsford, Essex, for Marconi. Paula left in Lisbon with her surviving paternal grandparents, whom she loved, and her mother's aunt, whom she did not. She considers this disruptive experience of great significance to her subversive tendencies as an artist.

1938 — Diagnosed as having incipient tuberculosis. Family moves to the seaside resort of Estoril, north of Lisbon.

1940–42 — Attends local primary school in Estoril.

1943–45 — Tutored at home by local teacher, Dona Violeta.

1945–51 — Attends St Julian's Anglican School, Carcavelos, the only English school in Portugal. Her talent for art is first noted and she gains an English School Certificate.

1951–52 — Attends The Grove, Sevenoaks, Kent, a finishing-school for girls, from which she discharges herself.

1952–56 — Attends the Slade School of Art, London, as an outside pupil. Shares first prize with David Storey, later famous as a novelist and dramatist, for her 1954 summer project painting, *Under Milk Wood*. Meets and falls in love with Victor Willing, who is married.

1956 — Birth of Caroline. Returns to Portugal.

1957 — Settles in Ericeira with Victor Willing and Caroline.

1959 — Victor Willing having gained a divorce, they marry Birth of Victoria in London. While in London is spurred to renewed efforts as a painter by seeing Dubuffet exhibition.

1961 — Their third child, Nicholas, is born. Starts working in collage and has three collage pictures accepted for 'Segunda Exposicao de Artes Plásticas', Calouste Gulbenkian Foundation, Lisbon.

1962 — Awarded two-year scholarship by Gulbenkian Foundation. Her works are shown for the first time in an exhibition of the London Group, then under the enterprising presidency of the painter Claude Rogers. Hockney, Andrews and Auerbach are among the fellow exhibitors. She and Vic buy terraced house in Albert Street, London NW1. Time now divided between London and Portugal.

1965 — Chosen by Roland Penrose for 'Six Artists' exhibition at the prestigious Institute of Contemporary Arts, London. First solo show, held at the Agleria de Arte Moderna in the Sociedade Nacional de Belas Artes, Lisbon. This was negotiated and introduced by her close friend the poet and essayist Alberto de Lacerda, and her first major public success.

1966 — Death of her father.

1967 — Vic diagnosed as having multiple sclerosis, a progressive disease of the nervous system.

1969 — Chosen to represent Portugal in the XI Bienal de São Paulo, Brazil.

1975 — Family electronic business is expropriated by workers as a result of the Portuguese revolution. Lengthy litigation with regard to compensation follows restoration of democracy and the return of law and order.

1976 — Establishes her permanent residence in London, travelling to Portugal only for holidays. Represents Portugal at XIII Bienal de São Paulo, Brazil. Takes time off painting to study children's illustration in British Museum, funded by a grant from the Gulbenkian Foundation.

1978 — Has eleven paintings in 'Portuguese Art since 1910' held at the Royal Academy of Arts, London. First solo show with Galeria III, Lisbon.

1979 — For economic reasons she is forced to sell the much loved *quinta* at Ericeira, which she always considered to be her true home.

1981 — First solo exhibition in London at the state-sponsored AIR Gallery. Rejects collage in favour of painting, with her *Red Monkey* series.

1982 Exhibits at the Edward Totah Gallery, her first solo exhibition at a private gallery in London.

1983 Visiting Lecturer in Painting at the Slade School of Art.
Work shown in USA for the first time: 'Eight in the Eighties' and 'Marathon 83', both in New York
'Paula Rego: Paintings 1982–83' (including *Opera* series) exhibited in London (Edward Totah), Bristol (Arnolfini) and Milan (Studio Marconi)

1984 Exhibits *Proles' Wall* commissioned for '1984 – An Exhibition' at Camden Arts Centre, London, in celebration of George Orwell's novel.

1985 Represents Great Britain at XVIII Bienal de São Paulo, with Stuart Brisley, Patrick Caulfield and John Davies.
Attends opening in Brazil.
Vivian Girl series.
First painting, *Nanny, Small Bears and Bogeyman*, 1983, enters collection of the Tate Gallery, London.
First solo show in the USA, held at The Art Palace, New York.

1987 'Selected work 1981–1986', a touring exhibition shown at Aberystwyth Arts Centre, Wales, and elsewhere in the UK.
Girl and Dog series exhibited at the Edward Totah Gallery.
Birth of Carmen Mueck, her first grandchild.
Paints *The Maids*.

1988 Death of Victor Willing.
Retrospective exhibition at the Gulbenkian Foundation, Lisbon and the Serpentine Gallery, London.
Is the subject of a television documentary 'The Artist's Eye', directed by Jake Auerbach (BBC Television).

1989 First solo show with Marlborough Fine Art, London: *Paula Rego: Nursery Rhymes*, printed by Paul Coldwell and first designed as a birthday present for Carmen.
The Dance (1988) purchased by Friends of the Tate Gallery, London, for the permanent collection.
Appointed Senior Fellow of the Royal College of Art.

1990 Appointed first Associate Artist of the National Gallery, London.
'Nursery Rhymes' exhibition toured nationally by state-sponsored South Bank Centre.
Birth of Lola Mueck.

1991 *Crivelli's Garden* mural unveiled as wall decoration in the brasserie of the new Sainsbury Wing, National Gallery, London making her the only living artist with a work on permanent display there.
'Tales from the National Gallery' opens its nationwide tour at Plymouth City Museum and Art Gallery.

1992 'Tales from the National Gallery' concludes nationwide tour at the National Gallery, London.
Television documentary 'Paula Rego' South Bank Show, directed by Melissa Raimes (London Weekend Television).
Presented with Honorary Degree by Winchester School of Art.

1993 First showing of *Dog Woman* together with earlier paintings and etchings from the Saatchi Collection – a mixed show with John Murphy and Avis Newman.
'Paula Rego, Dog Women', the series exhibited at Marlborough Fine Art, London.

1995 *Portrait of Germaine Greer* commissioned for 'New Acquisitions' by the National Portrait Gallery, London.

1996 Exhibited *Dancing Ostriches* together with paintings inspired by Disney's 'Snow White' and 'Pinocchio' in 'Spellbound: Art and Film' at the Hayward Gallery, London

SOLO EXHIBITIONS

1965 SNBA, Lisbon

1971 Galeria São Mamede, Lisbon

1972 Galeria Alvarez, Oporto

1974 Galeria da Emenda, Lisbon

1975 Módulo, Centro Difusor da Arte, Lisbon

1977 Módulo, Centro Difusor da Arte, Porto

1978 Galeria III, Lisbon

1981 AIR Gallery, London

1982 Galeria III, Lisbon
Edward Totah Gallery, London

1983 Arnolfini, Bristol
Galerie Espace, Amsterdam

1984 South Hill Park Arts Centre, Bracknell
Midland Group, Nottingham
Edward Totah Gallery, London

1985 The Art Palace, New York
Edward Totah Gallery, London

1987 'Selected Work 1981–1986', Aberystwyth Arts Centre and UK tour
Edward Totah Gallery, London

1988 Retrospective exhibition at the Fundação Calouste Gulbenkian, Lisbon, Casa de Serralves, Oporto, and the Serpentine Gallery, London

1989 'Paula Rego: Nursery Rhymes', Marlborough Graphics Gallery, London
Galeria III, ARCO, Madrid
Galeria III, Lisbon

1990 'Nursery Rhymes', Galeria III, Lisbon
'Nursery Rhymes', Galeria Zen, Oporto

1990–91 'Nursery Rhymes', British Council travelling exhibition in Europe

1991–92 'Tales from the National Gallery', travelling exhibition: Plymouth City Museum and Art Gallery; Middlesbrough Art Gallery; Whitworth Art Gallery, Manchester; Cooper Art Gallery, Barnsley; National Gallery, London; Laing Art Gallery, Newcastle; Calouste Gulbenkian Foundation, Lisbon

1991–96 'Nursery Rhymes', South Bank Centre travelling exhibition in the UK including: Bridport Arts Centre, Dorset; Rufford Craft Centre, Nottinghamshire; Hove Museum and Art Gallery; Vicarage Gallery, North Shields

1992–93 'Paula Rego: Peter Pan & Other Stories', Marlborough Fine Art, London
'Paula Rego: Peter Pan', A suite of 15 etchings and aquatints, Marlborough Graphics, London

1993 'Nursery Rhymes', Cheltenham Literary Festival

1994 'Paula Rego, Dog Women', Marlborough Fine Art (London) Ltd.
Art Gallery of Greater Victoria, Victoria BC, Canada

1995 'Nursery Rhymes', Ty Llen, Cardiff Literature Festival (May – July)
'Nursery Rhymes and Peter Pan', Annandale Galleries, Sydney, Australia; Charles Nodrum Gallery, Melbourne

1996 'Nursery Rhymes', University Gallery, University of Northumbria at Newcastle

GROUP EXHIBITIONS

1955 'Young Contemporaries', London

1961 'Segunda Exposiçao de Artes Plásticas', Fundaçao Calouste Gulbenkian, Lisbon

1965 'Six Artists', Institute of Contemporary Arts, London

1967 Bienal de Tokyo; 'Novas Iconologias', Lisbon
'Art Portugais – Peinture et sculpture de Naturalism à nos jours', Brussels, Paris, Madrid

1969 Represented Portugal in the XI Bienal de São Paulo, Brazil
'Gravure Portugaise Contemporaine', Paris

1970 'Novos Sintomas na pintura portuguesa Galeria, Judite Dacruz, Lisbon

1973 'Pintura portuguesa de hoje – abstractos e Neo-figurativos', Lisbon, Salamance, Barcelona
'26 Artistas de Hoje', Lisbon
'Exposiçao de Artistas Modernas Portugueses', Galeria Quandrum, Lisbon

1974 Expo AICA, SNBA

1975 XIII Bienal de São Paulo'Figuraçao Hoje', Lisbon

1976 'Arte Portugués Contemporanea', Galeria Nazionale d'Arte Moderna, Rome
'Art Portugais Contemporain' Musée d'Art Contemporain de la Ville de Paris
'Exposiçao de Arte Moderna Portuguesa', SNBA, Lisbon

1977 'Artistas Portugueses en Madrid – Pintura e Escultura Contemporaneas', Madrid

1978 'Portuguese Art since 1910', Royal Academy of Arts, London
Exposiçao individual, Galeria III, Lisbon

1979 'Femina', UNESCO, Paris

1981 'Artists in Camden', Camden Arts Centre, London
'Ante-visao do Centro de Arte Moderna', Fundaçao Calouste Gulbenkian, Lisbon
'The Subjective Eye', Midland Group, Nottingham

1982 'Three Women', Edward Totah Gallery, London
'Inner Worlds', Midland Group, Nottingham
'Pintura portugeusa contemporanea' Museu Luis de Camoes, Macao
'Hayward Annual', London
'John Moores Exhibition', Liverpool

1983 'Third Biennal of Graphic Arts', Baden-Baden
'Eight in the Eighties', New York
'Marathon 83', New York

1984 '1984 – an Exhibition', Camden Arts Centre, London
'Os Novos Primitivos', Cooperative Arvore, Oporto

1985 'The British Art Show', Ikon Gallery, Birmingham
'Diálogo sobre arte contemporanea', Centro de Arte Moderna; Fundaçao Calouste Gulbenkian, Lisbon
Bienal de Paris
'Animals', Edward Totah Gallery, London
'Exposiçao Diálogo', Fundaçao Calouste Gulbenkian, Lisbon
'John Moores Exhibition', Liverpool
Bienal de São Paulo (representing Britain)
'Passion and Power', La Mama and Gracie Mansion, New York

1986 'A primeira década', Módulo-Centro Difusor da Arte, Lisbon
'Le XXé au Portugal', Centre Albert Borchette, Brussels
'Terceira Exposiçao de Artes Plásticas', Fundaçao Calouste Gulbenkian, Lisbon
AICA-PHILAE, SNBA, Lisbon
'Love Sacred and Profane', Plymouth
'The Human Zoo', Nottingham Castle Museum, Nottingham
'Contemporary British and Malaysian Art', National Gallery, Kuala Lumpur
'Nove – Nine Portuguese Painters', John Hansard Gallery, Southampton

1987 'Art Contemporáneo Portugués', Madrid
'Current Affairs – British Painting and Sculpture in the 1980s', Museum of Modern Art, Oxford, Hungary, Poland and Czechoslovakia
'70–80: Arte Portugeusa', Brasilia, São Paulo, Rio de Janeiro
'Alberto da Lacerdo – O mundo de un poeta', Fundaçao Calouste Gulbenkian, Lisbon
'30 Obras de Arte Uniao de Bancos Portugeses', Casa de Serralves, Oporto
Feira do Circo, Forum Picoas, Lisbon
'Exposiçao Amadeo Souza-Cardoso', Casa de Serralves, Oporto
'Obras de uma Colecça Particular', Casa de Serralves, Oporto

1988 'Works on Paper by Contemporary Artists', Marlborough Fine Art, London
'35 Pinturas de Colecçao do Banco Portugues do Atlantico', Casa de Serralves, Oporto
'Cries and Whispers', British Council travelling exhibition, Australia
'Narrative Paintings', Castlefield Gallery, Manchester
'Objects and Images: Aspects of British Art in the 1980s', Stoke-on-Trent Art Gallery

1989 'Ines de Castro', Richard Demarco Gallery, Edinburgh

1989–90 'Picturing People: Figurative Art in Britain 1945–1989', British Council travelling exhibition: National Gallery, Kuala Lumpur, Hong Kong Museum of Art: National Gallery of Zimbabwe, Harare

1990 'Now for the Future', Hayward Gallery, London; Mappin Art Gallery, Sheffield
'Great Britain/USSR', British Council travelling exhibition, Kiev and Moscow
'Did You Ever See Such A Thing In Your Life?', Leeds City Art Gallery

1990–91 'British Art Now: A Subjective View', British Council travelling exhibition, Japan
'The Great British Art Exhibition', Glasgow
Eleventh International Print Biennale, Bradford

1991 Modern Painters – A Memorial Exhibition for Peter Fuller', City Art Galleries, Manchester
'Triptico', Museum van Hedendaagse Kunst, Ghent

1991–92 'From Bacon to Now – The Outsider in British Figuration', Palazzo Vecchio, Florence
'The Primacy of Drawing – An Artist's View', South Bank Centre travelling exhibition: Bristol Museum and Art gallery; Stoke-on-Trent Art Gallery; Graves Art Gallery, Sheffield

1992–93 'Life into Paint: British Figurative Painting of the 20th Century', Israel Museum, Jerusalem

1993–94 'Writing on the Wall – Women Writers on Women Artists', Tate Gallery, London, October 1993 – April 1994; travelling to the Norwich Castle Museum and the Arnolfini Gallery, Bristol

1994 'Unbound – Possibilities in Painting', Hayward Gallery, London
'Waves of Influence' (Nursery Rhymes and Peter Pan graphics), Snug Harbour Cultural Center, Statton Island, New York
'Here and Now', Serpentine Gallery, London
'John Murphy, Avis Newman, Paula Rego', The Saatchi Gallery, London
Contemporary Arts Society Art Market, Festival Hall, London

1994–95 'An American Passion – the Summer Collection of Contemporary British Painting', The McLellan Galleries, Glasgow; The Royal College of Art, London

1995 'Open Studio', The Florence Trust, London
'Summer Exhibition', Marlborough Fine Art, London
'Peep', Brighton Museum in collaboration with the Institute of International Visual Art
'New Acquisitions', National Portrait Gallery, London

1996 'David Hockney: Six Fairy Tales from the Brothers Grimm: Paula Rego: Nursery Rhymes', University Museum, Long Beach, California
'Spellbound: Art and Film', Hayward Gallery, London

Biography, Solo Exhibitions and Group Exhibitions reproduced with the kind permission of Phaidon Press Limited from their Paula Rego monograph by John McEwen, published in 1992.

Our thanks to Prudence Cuming and John Haynes for the use of photographic material.

Designed and published in 1996 by the Saatchi Gallery © 1996
98a Boundary Road, London NW8 0RH

Cover: detail of *Dancing Ostriches from Disney's 'Fantasia'* (7)
photograph courtesy Prudence Cuming © 1996

Printed by The Pale Green Press
Printed and bound in Great Britain

ISBN 0 9527 453 2 1